The Gentry & Aristocracy

Kilkenny

Cuffe of Desart

By

Art Kavanagh

2013

From the original printed in 2004

Preface

What matter that at different times
Our fathers won the sod
What matter if at different shrines
We pray to the one God
In fortune and in fame we're bound
By links as strong as steel
And neither shall be safe or sound
But in the other's weal
(*Thomas Davis*)

The story of Kilkenny is inextricably linked to the history of the Butlers, a family that stamped its mark not alone on Kilkenny but on the entire south east of Ireland. Today Kilkenny Castle stands as a monument to this remarkable family and Kilkenny city owes its existence to them. What was probably one of the most extraordinary facets of the Butlers was the fact that they were most prolific and their many sub branches included the Butlers of Mountgarret, the Butlers of Dunboyne, the Butlers of Carrick and numerous less well known branches such as the Butlers of Maidenhall. The fact that they managed to survive the Cromwellian carve up of Catholic lands is a tribute to their tenacity and intelligence.

The various Cromwellian families that settled in Kilkenny did so at the expense of families that were less powerful such as the Shees, the Rothes and the Shortalls and the remnants of the Gaelic families such as the FitzPatricks. Many of these new families such as the Agars of Gowran, the Ponsonbys of Pilltown and the Wandesfordes of Castlecomer left indelible marks in their areas and many fine golf courses and parks exist today because of their industry. The legacy of beautiful houses and well maintained demesnes has all but been lost. Fortunately, enough remain to ensure the continuity of settlement so vital to our understanding of history.

Other families to emerge such as the Smithwicks, the Bryans, the Powers, the Floods and the St. Georges gave Kilkenny many distinguished and talented men and women who contributed to the advancement of mankind not alone in Ireland but in other far flung lands

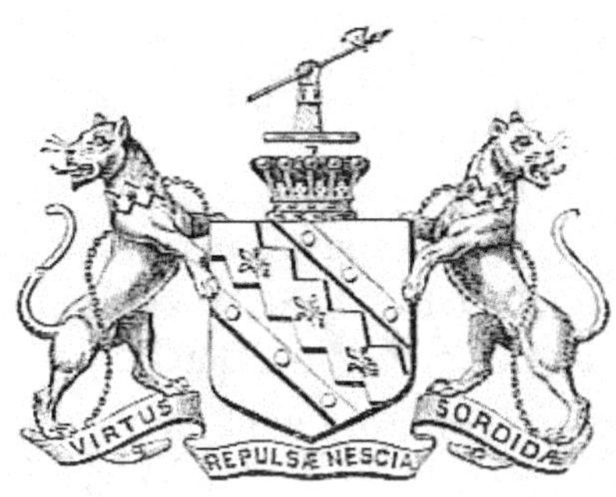

Cuffe of Desart

In 1921 the treaty between Britain and Ireland led to the establishment of the Irish Free State, which gave Ireland the right to govern itself as a Dominion within the British Empire. Within a few months, Ireland again erupted in conflict, this time a bitter civil war between the Provisional Government of the Irish Free State and those who felt that the Anglo-Irish Treaty fell far short of Republican ambitions.

On the night of February 1922, the 5th Earl of Desart was in London when a small group of Republicans walked up the avenue to Desart Court armed with fire-torches. Why it was felt necessary to destroy the building is unclear. The Desarts had not done anything obvious to bring this destruction upon them[1]. The 5th Earl had been amongst the earliest Irish landlords to agree to the sale of his estate in the wake of the 1903 Land Act. Lady Sybil Lubbock maintained the burning was "for no personal ill-will towards them [the Desarts] but in reprisal for some measure of severity on behalf of the new government". That same night, the Ponsonby's house at Bessborough was also

---

[1] Hubert Butler in his *Escape from the Anthill* seemed to think the attack was carried out to punish Senator Lady Desart for her political leanings. The houses of 37 Senators were burnt and in the following year 139 country houses were destroyed with their fine libraries, priceless antiques and marvellous potential.

burned. However, there does seem to have been an element of malicious intent in the burning, for, when a truck escaped from Desart carrying various pieces of furniture and art, it was apprehended at Athy and its contents destroyed. One can only guess at the treasures lost - the furniture, the portraits, the diaries, letters and correspondence. Ham Cuffe was distraught at the news. That so few of his tenants had lifted a finger to stop the destruction hurt him deeply. Ten years later, he wrote to his granddaughter, Iris Origo: "I can't bear to think of Desart -it is sadness itself. All gone, all scattered - and we were so happy there". He never again returned to Ireland

In 1641, Hugh Cuffe's grandson, the Ennis-born Joseph Cuffe, joined a cavalry regiment raised to defend the interests of the new planters during what would become one of the most brutal wars in Irish history. During Oliver Cromwell's Protectorate, Sir Charles Coote, a first cousin of Joseph, became one of the most powerful men in Ireland. Another close family friend was Sir William Petty, the man entrusted with the redistribution of lands confiscated from Catholic Irish families to English officers. In 1654, Joseph Cuffe was awarded a substantial 5000 acre estate in the barony of Shillelogher, County Kilkenny. In due course his descendents would come to call the estate "Desart".[2] When a serious challenge to the Cromwellian land settlement was initiated by the administration of the Catholic James II, Agmondesham Cuffe, Joseph's son and heir, was amongst the first men to take up his sword for the Dutch Prince William of Orange.[3]

---

[2] In the twelfth century, Earl William Marshal granted the parish of Castleinch to the Anglo-Norman De Valle (or Wall) family. By the 17th century, Shillelogher was one of the wealthiest baronies in the country, held in the patrimony of the Earl of Ormond. In the 1640s the resident landholder, Gerald Comerford of Castleinch hosted Archbishop Rinuccini, the Papal Nuncio, before he entered Kilkenny City to meet with the Irish confederates there. In 1650 Kilkenny surrendered to Cromwell's forces, and in 1654 Gerald Comerford was attainted for treason. His castle and lands at Castleinch were forfeited to Joseph Cuffe, Esq. Following the restoration of Charles II, and the death of Sir Charles Coote in 1661, the Comerfords, perhaps encouraged by their friendship with the Duke of Ormonde, successfully appealed the forfeiture of their estates. Under the Act of Settlement & Explanation, Joseph Cuffe was granted 200 plantation acres including 1200 acres at "Tullaghane, to be called and known for ever by the name of Cuffe's Desart. In total his estate in Kilkenny came to 5425 acres, including 324 acres at Cuffe's Grange and 420 acres in Killaloe. See Ronald P. Larkin, *The Road to Knockeenbaun*, Kilmanagh. (2002), p. 46.

[3] Among the family portraits that perished during the burning of Desart Court in 1922 was an oil in good condition, of a man believed to have been Agmondesham Cuffe. The artist was reputed to have been the Dutch artist, Sir Godfrey Kneller.

The victory of the Williamite forces over the Irish Catholics was in many ways absolute. It set in motion an age where the new Protestant elite was able to settle down and develop the hitherto unruly island into a proper English colony.

Perhaps the greatest symbols of the age of the Protestant Ascendancy were the enormous mansions erected by individual landowners across the country. Desart Court was amongst the earliest such constructions. It was built on the Cuffe family estate in Kilkenny in 1733 for John Cuffe, later 1st Lord Desart, eldest son of Agmondesham Cuffe, the Williamite soldier.

Desart Court

A graduate of Trinity College Dublin, John Cuffe stood as MP for Thomastown, County Kilkenny, from 1715 to 1727. Desart Court has been described as one of Ireland's most outstanding architectural triumphs. Its original architect is increasingly believed to have been Sir Edward Lovett Pearce, the man who designed Parliament House in Dublin. The construction costs appear to have been partially met through the sale of a large quantity of silver plate seized during a raid on the French fortress of Quebec by the father-in-law of the 1st Lord Desart.[4]

Agmondesham's son, John, was educated at Kilkenny College where Jonathan Swift had studied a decade earlier.[5] Like Swift and his father before him, John Cuffe went on to study at Trinity College Dublin, founded just over a century earlier by Queen Elizabeth. He entered Trinity aged 14 on 7th August 1697, became a Fellow Commoner and graduated with a Bachelor of Arts in 1701. It was during this period that the Rubrics, the oldest surviving building in the college today, was built.

His brother, Maurice, was called to the Irish Bar in 1712, became a King's Counselor for four years and represented the City of Kilkenny in King George I's Irish Parliament from 1715 to 1726. In 1732 he built a house at Killaghy (or St. Alban's) near the Ballyspellin Spa in County Kilkenny. He married Martha Fitzgerald, daughter of John Fitzgerald of Ballymaloe, Co. Cork.[6] A third brother was Denny Cuffe, MP, who married Grace Wright of Dublin and was ancestor of the Wheeler-Cuffe family. There was also a daughter, Martha, who married John Blunden, MP, father of Sir John Blunden, 1st Bart.[7]

---

[4] In her recollections, Dorothea Herbert, grand-daughter of John Cuffe, wrote that the marriage settlement between her grandparents had included "ten thousand pounds worth of plate, taken by her father [i.e.: General Gorges] at the Siege of Quebec". However, as the Siege did not take place until 1759, this may be a mistake. Perhaps Gorges acquired the fortune during the English raids on the French fortress of Quebec in the 1690s.

[5] Alumni Dublinenses, Burtchell & Sadlier, Royal Irish Academy, 2001 reprint, Vol. 1, p.200.

[6] Maurice and Martha's daughter Anne (Nancy) Cuffe was, for a short time, the wife of Edmond Fitzgerald, 20th Knight of Glin, (1705 - 1773), a member of the notorious Hell Fire Club. Born in February 1721, she was the second of seven daughters. A contemporary described her as 'a popular Protestant beauty from Kilkenny'. It is thus a surprise that her husband, whom she married in March 1740, was the still Catholic Knight of Glin. For reasons unknown - perhaps the Knight's mounting gambling debts - the marriage was a failure. She subsequently married her second cousin, as his second wife, Denny Baker Cuffe of Cuffesborough, King's County (modern Offaly) but died soon after on 24th October 1776.

[7] Sir John seems to have been a difficult man. His niece, Dorothea Herbert, recalled how he let none of his sons go to a public school and "kept his beautiful daughters shut up in a nursery making lace under an old Governess and their Mammy nurse until they were 15 or 16". When he died in January 1783, Sir John's will expressed the memorable wish "that he may not be buried till his head begins to be putrefied or his head severed from his body, and laid without ceremony in the round part of the wood

John Cuffe's political career commenced in 1708, when, at the age of 25, he was appointed Sheriff of Kilkenny. Seven years later he began to make his mark in the Irish House of Commons when he became MP for Thomastown, a position he retained for 12 years from the accession of King George I in 1715 to the accession of King George II in 1727.[8] As to his character, we have a description by his granddaughter Dorothea Herbert who recalled him as "a remarkably handsome and good man".

His first wife, Margaret Hamilton, from County Down died childless and young and in 1726, John Cuffe married again. His second wife - the future 1st Lady Desart - was Dorothea Gorges.[9]

Within a year of John and Dorothea's marriage both their fathers and King George I were dead. So too was John's sister, Martha Blunden. As heir to Agmondesham Cuffe, John and his wife then moved to the family estate at Castleinch in County Kilkenny. Over the next twelve years, Dorothea bore her husband nine children, of whom seven survived childhood. In between all this, she spent her time weaving a tapestry representing the Rising Sun which her granddaughter, Dorothea Herbert, recalled seeing on a visit to Desart in 1773.

Perhaps it was the noise of so many children in his home or more likely it was the growing pretensions of the landed gentry that, in 1733, inspired John Cuffe to abandon the old tower house of Castleinch and commission the construction of a new country manor which he would call Desart Court.[10]

---

where the laurel is planted and the ditch of water surrounds it". The Castleblunden estate contained "a highly romantic mid 18th century house with water on both sides of it so that it seems to float", built just outside Kilkenny City by Sir John. (Bence-Jones, 1988, p. 63).

[8] One of his contemporaries at Kilkenny College and sometime neighbour was the philosopher, Bishop George Berkeley, who was born at Dysart (not to be confused with Desart) Castle outside Thomastown in 1685. Berkeley achieved much fame when he visited the American colonies with the novel idea of establishing schools for "the instruction of the youth of America". His memory is enshrined in the name of Berkeley College, California.

[9] Through her mother Dorothea was connected with the Beresfords and the Powers of Curraghmore (the Earls of Tyrone after 1690). Marcus Beresford, Dorothea's half brother, who inherited Curraghmore, was created Earl of Tyrone in 1746. Her father, an Army officer from Co. Meath, went on to become a General. Her younger sister was married to William St. Lawrence, Lord Howth. Relationships between the families of Gorges and St. Lawrence must have come asunder in 1736 when Hamilton Gorges, brother to both Lady Desart and Lady Howth, killed Lord Howth's brother in a duel.

[10] Said to have been designed by Sir Edward Lovett Pearce (1699 - 1733) who was the architect for the stunning new Parliament House.

At any rate, Desart Court was built and was a classic example of early Georgian construction. It was built with blue limestone and comprised a central block with pavilions projecting on either side. Over the ensuing decades, the interior was fitted with sumptuous tapestries, oil paintings by Italian Masters, Chippendale chairs, dado wood paneling, rococo ceilings, Dutch walnut cabinets, bookcases "enriched with fluted pilasters", beautifully carved Oakwood balustrades and mantelpieces from Sienna. The Cuffe family fortunes were substantially reduced in the process.

Desart Court – rear

John Cuffe may have been fretting about the unpaid bills involved in the construction of his new stately home but he must also have derived considerable pleasure when, on 10th November 1733, he was elevated to the peerage as Baron Desart of Desart in the Irish Peerage. The preamble to the patent applauded his father and grandfather; particularly the latter's efforts to ensure the "Protestant succession".[11] He took his seat in the Irish House of

---

[11] Quoted in The Complete Peerage, GEC, but also in Lodge, Vol. VI.

Lords two days later, no doubt casting a nod at his brother-in-law, Lord Howth, seated opposite.

Lord Desart further indebted himself in 1735 with the purchase of the Ormond Estate at Callan from Charles Butler, Earl of Arran, for £11,120. Thirty years later his son was compelled to sell some 2000 acres of the Callan lands to pay off the family debts[12].

John Cuffe, 1st Lord Desart, died on 26th June 1749 and was buried alongside his father and grandfather at the Church of Inchiholaghan in Castleinch. He was succeeded by his eldest son, 19 year old John Cuffe, 2nd Baron Desart, then a student at Trinity College, Dublin.

His wife, the Dowager Lady Dorothea Desart, survived him for nearly eighteen years, finally succumbing "at her house in Henry Street" in 1777. Her daughter Susanna was married off to her first cousin, Sir John Blunden, son of the 1st Lord Desart's sister Martha. It was Sir John who built the original house at Castleblunden, perhaps seeking to emulate his father-in-law's creation at Desart Court. The second daughter Sophia was given to a Killarney-born lawyer named John Herbert and the third, Martha, to his brother, the Reverend Nicholas Herbert.[13]

With regard to Lady Dorothea Desart's sons, the eldest, John, 2nd Lord Desart, went to Trinity College Dublin and married a Cork heiress but predeceased her by 10 years. The second son, Otway, 3rd Lord Desart, later 1st Earl of Desart, was dispatched across the sea to Christ Church College, Oxford, and became a lawyer. As befitting the age, the third son, Hamilton, joined the church whilst the fourth, William, secured a commission in the army with the 17th Dragoons.

Known to his Irish contemporaries as "Sean an Chaipin", John Cuffe, 2nd Baron Desart was born on 16th November 1730, the eldest surviving son of John and Dorothea Cuffe. Like his father, John was educated at Trinity College Dublin. He had not long entered the college when his father died on 26th June 1749. Thus, at the age of 19, John succeeded as 2nd Lord Desart, an inheritance that brought with it one of the grandest country houses in Ireland. Showing every bit as much political pluck as his forbears, the 2nd Baron took his seat in the House of Lords on 25th November 1751, 9 days after his 21st birthday.

On September 2nd 1752 this most eligible of bachelors took as his bride a young widow from County Cork, Sophia Thornhill.[14]

---

[12] The purchaser was James Agar of Ringwood (see chapter 1 for details of that family)

[13] Dorothea Herbert's father

[14] Her husband was Richard Thornhill of St. Stephen's Green. Dublin. Her father was a wealthy landowner named Bettridge Badham of Rockfield, County Cork. Her mother

The 2nd Lord Desart and his wife, Lady Sophia, had three daughters. Sophia married Richard Cooke in June 1772; Catherine married Sir Charles Burton, of Pollerton, County Carlow, in August 1778 and Lucy married William Weldon in May 1792. These were first cousins of Dorothea Herbert and she has left us with this insight into the lives of the three sisters: "Mrs. Cooke was as good a Creature as possible but had a couple of Mischief making Servants who constantly tattled and put her out of Temper. She was a fine figure of a woman, large and handsome, though not so beautiful as her sister, Lady Burton, whom she greatly resembled. These two and Mrs. Weldon were co-heiresses to the late Lord Desart's alienable property." [15] Sophia was the Mrs. Cooke, mentioned by her relative Dorothea Herbert, who, when her husband died, painted all the flowerpots black, reupholstered the furniture in sable and tarred the stables turning an elderly visitor's horses piebald 'for which he whipped the stableboy.'

The 2nd Lord Desart was not a particularly wealthy man. His father had spent a considerable portion of the family fortunes on the construction of Desart and the purchase of the Callan estates from the Earl of Arran. In 1765 he sold 2,108 acres of this estate, including the town of Callan, to James Agar, sometime MP of Kilkenny.[16]

John Cuffe, 2nd Lord Desart died at Desart at the relatively young age of 37 on 25th November 1767, sixteen years to the day after he first took his seat in the House of Lords.[17]

---

was Sophia King, daughter of John King, 3rd Baron Kingston (1664 - 1728) and his wife "a pretty and persistent Irish scullery maid". It was while living at the King family's new house of Rockingham near Boyle in County Roscommon that the future 3rd Baron Kingston first developed "a more than ordinary and suspicious familiarity" with Margaret (Peggy) O'Cahan. By the time his elder brother, Robert, 2nd Baron Kingston, heard of the romance the "amour was well advanced" and the couple had married. The 3rd Baron's uncle captured the essence of the King family reaction to the marriage in this manner: "Few of the nobility of English extraction have ever contracted marriages with Irish papists but none (up to this case) have married one who was at once an ordinary Servant Maid and an Irish Papist who had neither Charms of Beauty nor genteel behaviour nor agreeableness of conversation".

[15] In addition to these three girls, the 2nd Lord Desart recognised an illegitimate son, Joseph Cuffe who was packed off to live with the Herberts though the family "respected and loved him as much as if he had been Legitimated into it".

[16] See Chapter 1.

[17] James Hoban, the celebrated architect of the White House in the U.S.A. was born on the Desart estate during the lifetime of the 2nd Lord. Hoban had been born in 1762, in one of the tenant cottages at Desart, and educated in the estate school established by the 2nd Lord Desart. Showing much prowess at drawing, young Hoban then moved

Otway Cuffe was the second surviving son of John and Dorothea Cuffe. Four weeks after his brother's demise, he took his seat in the Irish House of Lords. He was educated at Christ Church College, Oxford. He was the first of his family to have studied at that University since Henry Cuffe, the Elizabethan gentleman executed with the Earl of Essex 150 years earlier. Over the next 150 years, Christ Church was to be the destination for a number of his sons, grandsons and great-grandsons.

Stairway – Desart Court

Otway appears to have been an enlightened individual who did much to enhance the state of County Kilkenny during his time at Desart. In this regard he must have been much aided by a new high road, commenced in 1750, which linked Kilkenny and Callan. This formed the principal entrance into the city of Kilkenny from the numerous mansions of the Anglo-Irish families in the south and southwestern parts of the county. The 3rd Lord Desart stood as Mayor of Kilkenny from 1771 to 1772 and again from 1779 and 1780. During this time he introduced street-lighting and "scavenging" (i.e.: rubbish collecting) programmes to the city and, in 1773, oversaw the restructuring of the Linen Market there. His interest in horse racing was such that, in 1767, he was appointed Steward of the Kilkenny Races.

---

from Kilkenny to school in Dublin where he was awarded the prestigious Duke of Leinster's medal by the Dublin Society. He subsequently served as an apprentice to the Cork-born architect Thomas Ivory who, later worked on redesigning Westport House for the 3rd Lady Desart's father.

On 6th January 1781, Otway Cuffe was "advanced to the dignity" of Viscount Desart, probably in recognition of his political influence as patron of half the borough of Kilkenny. Four years later, he married 30-year-old Lady Anne Browne. Lady Anne was a wealthy lady 25 years his junior. The Brownes, Earls of Altamont, descended from the great Pirate Queen, Grace O'Malley.[18] Lady Anne Browne's parents were, Peter Brown, 2nd Earl of Altamont, who in 1752 married Elizabeth Kelly, heiress to one of the largest Jamaican sugar plantations.

In 1785 the marriage of Otway Cuffe to Lady Anne Browne must have brought a considerable fortune to the House of Desart. It also afforded them an intimate association with one of the great families in Ireland.[19] On 20th February 1788 Lady Desart bore her elderly husband a son and heir, Otway Cuffe the younger, later 2nd Earl of Desart. Lady Desart also produced two daughters - Lady Dorothea and Lady Elizabeth.

In the 18th Century the rise of the Protestant Ascendancy, and the growth of landlord's economic and political power, inevitably affected relations between landlords and tenants. Many tenants responded aggressively to specific issues including the enclosure of common land and payment of tithes on crops, and by the second half of the 18th Century agrarian violence had become a feature of life in the Irish countryside. By 1761 a movement known as the Whiteboys (they wore white shirts over their everyday clothes), began to mobilise by night in counties Tipperary and Kilkenny. Their methods of protest included the houghing of animals, destroying fences erected around the large estates, and intimidation of the despised tithe collectors. Although in succeeding decades, several Acts were passed through Parliament to control such outrages, there was a fresh outbreak or violence in 1791. Viscount Desart

---

[18] John Browne, 1st Earl of Altamont, also commissioned the eminent German architect Richard Cassells (or Castle) to build a new house for his family at Westport on Clew Bay.

[19] Anne's brother, John Browne, 3rd Earl of Altamont, succeeded to the title on the death of their father in 1780. Only 24 years old at the time, he was already regarded as one of the wealthiest men in the land. One of his father's last acts before his death had been to employ the architect Thomas Ivory to substantially enlarge the original Westport House (1776 – 1778). In 1781, the 3rd Earl continued the family trend by commissioning James Wyatt to design a town around the Atlantic port in order to encourage the development of the local linen industry. Two years later, in May 1787, the Earl of Altamont married Louisa Howe, youngest daughter of the celebrated Admiral Howe, later created 1st Earl of Howe, as a result of his famous victory over the French revolutionary fleet on 1 June 1794.

appears also to have been affected by this crisis, as in that year, he and his cousin George Beresford, Marquess of Waterford, mustered a force of Protestant militia and spent several months stamping out this form of protest in the area.[20]

On 4th December 1793 Otway Cuffe was elevated in the Irish Peerage as Earl of Desart. In addition he was made Viscount Castle-cuff, a junior title subsequently borne by his first-born son and heir. Otway Cuffe took his seat as Earl of Desart in the Irish House of Lords the following January.

The revolt of the United Irishmen - better known as the 1798 Rebellion - which was ultimately a disaster and a tragedy, had little impact in Kilkenny and even less on the Desart estate.

What it did in fact achieve was the arousal of much fear in the hearts of the Ascendancy. It also encouraged the British Parliament in London to view Ireland less as a self-sufficient province and more as a potential base from which Napoleon Bonaparte could launch an attack on England's western flank.

In 1800 the Irish Parliament voted itself out of existence and ceased to exist, an event formalised by the 1801 Act of Union. Ireland's five million strong population now found themselves in a situation where all major decisions on Irish affairs were henceforth to be concluded at Westminster, a situation that remained until independence was granted to the Irish Free State in 1921. There had initially been strong opposition to the Act from the Anglo-Irish elite but many found themselves re-evaluating their position when London offered substantial "compensation" to those of a wavering disposition.[21]

Discontent amongst the aristocracy was further quelled by the reassurance that their order - the peerage - would continue to exert an influence in London through the 28 "Representative Peers of Ireland" in the British House of Lords, of whom the 1st Earl of Desart was one. The 3rd, 4th and 5th Earls would also subsequently hold this honour. The 3rd Earl of Desart was possibly the first of his family to spend long periods of time in London, in order to occupy his seat in the House of Lords, and participate in the festivities of the Season. Most "Backwoods Peers" hired apartments or purchased houses

---

[20] Otway's youngest brother, William Cuffe, a Major in the British Army, died of a fever while serving with the garrison at Athlone in 1790. Dorothea Herbert recalled him as a "headstrong and hot" man who caused much trouble in his youth with his argumentative nature. A portrait of him by Johan Zoffany was among those destroyed in the 1922 fire at Desart Court.

[21] Among the beneficiaries was the 1st Earl of Desart's brother-in-law, the Earl of Altamont, who was created Marquis of Sligo on 29th December 1800.

for such periods, although when the 67-year-old 1st Earl died on 9th August 1804, his death took place at his house in Kildare Street, Dublin. He was succeeded by his 16-year-old son, Otway, Viscount Castle-Cuffe, then a school boy at Eton.

The 1st Earl's wife, Anne, Countess of Desart, survived her husband by ten years, before she succumbed to a "nervous fever" in 1814.

Otway Cuffe, 2nd Earl of Desart, had a short but eventful life. He was born in Dublin on 20th February 1788, the only son and heir of the then Lord and Lady Desart. Like his father before him, he studied at Christ Church, Oxford, matriculating on 29th April 1805. Another man who matriculated from Oxford that year became his good friend: (Sir) Robert Peel, a former Harrovian who would later become Prime Minister of Great Britain.

The 2nd Earl had two sisters - Elizabeth and Dorothea. The first married Henry Wemyss of Danesfort, County Kilkenny, and had a son, Otway Wemyss, who served with the Buffs (The Royal East Kent Regiment). Her great-nephew, Hamilton Cuffe, 5th Earl of Desart, recalled her as "a sort of cross between a housekeeper and a Grand Duchess [who] might have come straight out of the pictures in a Dickens's book." He described the second sister, his great-aunt Lady Dorothea, as "a very different type ... rather like an eagle, and very formidable and determined".[22]

Unlike his father, the 2nd Earl was not one of the Representative Peers sent to represent Ireland in Westminster. However, this did not preclude him from politics and, from 1808 to 1817, he stood as Tory MP for Bossiney in Cornwall, once the seat of Sir Francis Drake, and apparently the place in which King Arthur's Hall of Chivalry supposedly lay. In 1809 he accepted a post as Lord of the Treasury under Lord Portland's Tory government, which he retained until 1810. During that year he also stood as Mayor of Kilkenny, a city on the rise following its Georgian re-construction, which included the Club House Hotel built three years earlier.

On 7th October 1817 the 2nd Earl of Desart married 18-year-old Catherine O'Connor. She was perhaps a curious choice for the Earl of Desart for she hailed from one of the most ancient Celtic bloodlines in Ireland. In time this would ferment itself in the mind of her youngest grandson, Otway Cuffe, one of the leading proponents of the Gaelic Revival in Ireland. Born shortly after the conclusion of the 1798 Rebellion, Catherine was the eldest daughter

---

[22] Her husband, Major General Sir James Campbell, KCB, had served in the Peninsular War under the Duke of Wellington, and later as Governor of Ceylon. Their marriage was an unhappy affair, made considerably worse when - in the face of a Chancery court order awarding custody of their four pretty daughters to their father Sir James - Lady Dorothea fled to France and kept the unfortunate girls there, for the next 15 years.

and co heiress of Maurice and Maria Nugent O'Connor of Gortnamona (or Mount Pleasant) in the "King's County" (i.e.: County Offaly). Her great-grandfather, Maurice O'Connor, "heir to the principality of Ofelia", had been amongst the first of the Irish Catholics to conform to Protestantism in the wake of Cromwell's invasion and having earned himself a fortune at the bar in England, married a daughter of the Earl of Fingall.

Her father had been a prominent advocate of Roman Catholic Emancipation and on a lesser level was a celebrated breeder of red setters, establishing a kennel at Gortnamona in 1779. The setters from this kennel were considered amongst the highest quality gun-dogs in the British Isles.[23] However, the 2nd Earl cannot have had much time to discuss the hazards of emancipation or indeed of shooting dogs for within a year of his marriage to Catherine, his new father-in-law lay dead.[24]

Catherine's mother was Maria Burke, the eldest daughter of Sir Thomas Burke of Marble Hill, County Galway.[25] These then were the aunts and uncles of Catherine, Countess of Desart. The influence they may have had over her is unknown but it is surely relevant, for instance, that her "Uncle

---

[23] The bloodline was later transferred to the La Touche family of Harristown, Co. Kildare, after the marriage to one of the O'Connor daughters. It stayed at Harristown until the 1860s when sold at auction to Sir A. Chichester of Devonshire. The Cuffes were linked to dog breeding on several other occasions. The 3rd Earl of Desart's kinsman, the Duke of Buccleuch, pioneered the importation of Labradors in the 1830s. Lady Kathleen Pilkington, only daughter of the 4th Earl of Desart, is likewise credited with the boom in French bulldogs across London during the reign of Edward VII.

[24] Unusually, Gortnamona then devolved upon Maurice Nugent O'Connor's youngest daughter, Elizabeth, who married the Reverend Benjamin Morris. Their son, William O'Connor Morris (1824 - 1904) was one of the great Judges of the Irish Supreme Court in Queen Victoria's reign. Like Desart, the house was burned down by the IRA in 1922

[25] Among the family portraits destroyed in the 1922 burning of Desart Court were oil paintings of the 2nd Earl of Desart and his wife by the Irish portrait artist Thomas Clement Thompson, and of both Maurice and Maria Nugent O'Connor. Thompson's two pictures were exhibited at the Royal Academy in 1819. Sir Thomas must have been a man of much ambition for Maria was one of four daughters that married into the upper realms of the British aristocracy. In 1799, Maria's sister Elizabeth married John de Burgh, Earl of Clanricarde (1744 - 1808). Their daughter Hester would go on to marry the enigmatic Marquess of Sligo while a great-granddaughter, Margaret, would take up residence at Desart Court as the Countess of Desart. In April 1806, Maria's youngest sister, Anne, married Sir Henry Tichborne (1779 - 1845), a direct descendent of the man who first proclaimed the accession of James I to the crown of England on the death of Queen Elizabeth. The third sister married Percy Clinton Smythe, 6th Viscount Strangford and 1st Baron Penshurst (1780 - 1855).

Percy" taught George IV how to sail and that, in 1852, his son, the 7th Viscount Strangford, a member of Benjamin Disraeli's "Young England" group, fought the last duel in England against Colonel Frederick Romilly.

Drawing Room at Desart Court

In the autumn of 1818, Catherine bore a son and heir, John Otway O'Connor Cuffe, Viscount Castle-Cuffe, delivered at Desart. Happiness should have followed but, alas, on 23rd November 1820 the 2nd Earl died at Desart. He was 33 years old. Had he lived on, he would almost certainly have become a well known figure in Parliament. Aside from his intimate friendship with Peel, he was also a close colleague of Spencer Perceval, the British Prime Minister assassinated in 1812 by John Bellingham - a failed businessman from Liverpool, who blamed the Tory politician for his financial difficulties.[26]

The Countess married again in 1826 and again misfortune befell her. Her second husband died after less than two years. Catherine, herself, lived until 1874. She died in Dublin in the family home on Pembroke Road.

John Otway O'Connor Cuffe, 3rd Earl of Desart was born on 17th October 1818. As a young infant, he was styled Viscount Castle-Cuffe, until his father's death on 23rd November 1820, at which time he succeeded to Desart Court and the Earldom at the age of two years.

---

[26] 55 A portrait of Spencer Perceval painted from a mask taken after his death was amongst those destroyed in the 1922 fire at Desart Court. It was painted by G.F. Joseph, ARA, and presented to the 2nd Earl in 1813.

In 1830 John followed in his father's footsteps and went to Eton where he stayed until 1834.[27] He would thus have been far away from Kilkenny when "distressing riots" broke out over the payment of tithes in the early 1830s.

The 3rd Earl of Desart married Lady Elizabeth Campbell, third daughter of the Earl of Cawdor and granddaughter of the 2nd Marquess of Bath.

In marrying Lady Elizabeth Campbell, the Earl of Desart brought his family into close contact with the leading Society figures during a time when Great Britain was establishing itself as the most powerful empire on the planet. His wife was closely related - if not by blood, then by marriage - to the Dukes of Abercorn, Bedford, Bridgewater, Buccleuch, Devonshire and Rutland, the Marquess of Bath, the Earls of Cawdor, Carlisle, Ellesmere, Galloway and Harewood, and the Viscounts Torrington and Weymouth.

The young couple enjoyed the Queen's patronage. In 1845 the young wife was invited to be a Lady of the Bedchamber to Victoria, a position she retained until 1864.[28] The 3rd Earl must have been delighted with the appointment for it gave him an excuse to join his wife when she was in attendance upon Her Majesty at the Royal retreat of Osborne House in the Isle of Wight. A keen yachtsman, the 3rd Earl spent much time at Cowes where he and his young sons sailed and boated with the Royal family.

During the 1850s, the 3rd Earl began to pay close heed to the goings on at Desart, and it is there, in Kilkenny that his four children had their most powerful childhood memories. A daughter, Alice, was born in 1844. A son and heir, William Ulick O'Connor Cuffe, was born at Grosvenor Crescent on 10th July 1845. A "spare heir", Hamilton Cuffe, followed on 30th August 1848[29] and a "spare spare", Otway Cuffe, concluded the batch in 1853. The second son, Hamilton, recalled his childhood at Desart as "a permanent delight".

The year of William's birth coincided with the first year of the potato blight in Ireland, an event that heralded the worst famine to hit Western Europe for several centuries, and which reduced the population of Ireland by over two million in less than a decade.[30] Like many of his peers the Earl was largely absent from Ireland during the famine years and like most of them he gave generously to the various Relief Committees set up to alleviate the sufferings

---

[27] Among his classmates at Eton was the future Crimean war soldier Colonel Lord Henry Percy (1817-1877) who won a VC at Inkerman in 1854.

[28] Ladies-in-Waiting, From the Tudors to the Present Day, by Anne Somerset (1984)

[29] In 1848 the 3rd Earl commissioned Henry Richard Graves (1818-1882) to paint his portrait. This was yet another of the family portraits destroyed in the 1922 fire.

[30] One of the more uplifting examples set by the landed gentry during the Famine was set by the 3rd Earl's half-sister, Maria, and her new husband, John la Touche. They culled their herd of deer at Harristown and fed the venison to their tenants.

of the poor. As already mentioned Kilkenny people were not so badly affected by the famine. Landlords were affected in that they had to forego or reduce rents in certain circumstances.

By the time that William joined the Grenadier Guards in 1862, tensions between the Federal States of America and Great Britain had been escalating for several years. The regiment was duly dispatched, along with the Scots Fusiliers, to shore up British defenses in Canada. William's younger brother and eventual heir Ham Cuffe also headed across the Atlantic at this time, as a Midshipman on board the wooden frigate, Orlando. The Grenadiers remained in Canada after the outbreak of the American Civil War later that year. William had attained the rank of Captain when, in the early spring of 1865, he was summoned back to London to attend upon his dying father. The 3rd Earl had been out hunting with the Kilkenny Hounds when he took a serious fall, compounding a spinal injury he had earlier sustained yachting in Greece. His wife, Lady Elizabeth, rushed him back to the doctors in London but a fatal paralysis had already set in and, on 1st April the 46-year-old died at his residence on Eaton Square.

William "Willie" Ulick O'Connor Cuffe lived for 53 years and was 4th Earl of Desart for 33 of them. In public life, he appears to have been much given to the leisurely pursuits of yachting and hunting so popular with the upper class in the late Victorian age, complimented by a penchant for writing mystery thrillers. His private life was a more complex affair, involving two very different marriages - the first to a great-granddaughter of Lord Edward Fitzgerald, the second to the Jewish heiress, Ellen Bischoffsheim.

The 4th Earl's first marriage of 1871 was an unhappy affair. His bride, Maria Emma Preston, was of a flighty disposition. Her grandmother was "Little Pam", daughter of Lord Edward Fitzgerald, the Irish revolutionary killed in the early days of the 1798 struggle, and the beautiful Pamela Fitzgerald, reputed daughter of the egalitarian Duke of Orleans. Her grandfather, Major General Sir Guy Campbell (1786 - 1849) was one of the great heroes of Waterloo and later commanded the 3rd West India Regiment.[31]

---

[31] A contemporary recalled the courtship of Sir Guy and Little Pam thus: "Sir Guy, when a young officer, was at a fete where Pamela's daughter was present. A young man, one of the guests, called out to the band to play "Croppies Lie Down". Campbell conceiving the request to be intended as an insult to Miss Fitzgerald demanded an immediate apology from the young man. I remember, so far, the story, but whether an apology was made or a duel ensued I cannot recollect, but I often heard that Miss Fitzgerald was so pleased with the action of the young officer that she said if ever she got married it would be to the gentleman who championed her on that occasion".

Maria gave birth to the 4th Earl's only child, a daughter, Lady Kathleen Mary Alexina Cuffe the year following the wedding. The marriage came asunder in the early months of 1878 when the young Countess of Desart was revealed to have indulged in an affair with the Shakespearean stage actor, Charles Sugden.[32] The Desarts were divorced in May 1878, and Maria married her lover at the British Embassy in Paris the following 26th December. That same year, Prime Minister Disraeli appointed the 4th Earl's brother, Hamilton Cuffe, Assistant Solicitor to the Treasury.

Although the 4th Earl's second marriage to Ellen Bischoffsheim produced no children, the marriage was an infinitely more satisfactory affair, bringing the House of Desart into intimate contact with one of the richest families in Europe.

It was hailed as the wedding of the Season. Rumours abounded that the Jewish bride brought a dowry of £150,000 with her, a similar sum being due on the death of her father. Before the year was out, the 4th Earl was appointed Master of the Kilkenny Foxhounds.

Reminiscences of Sir Charles Cameron, CB, Dublin; Hodges, Figgis & Co., Ltd. (1913).

[32] Charles Sudgen was born circa 1851 and died on the 3rd August 1921. He was perhaps an awkward man for, on 1st May 1891, his wife, the former Countess of Desart, was obliged to obtain a decree nisi against him. He performed as Bernardo in "Hamlet" (London Adelphi, June 1868), as Touchstone to Lily Langtry's Rosalind in "As You Like It" (St. James's Theatre, Feb - April 1890) and as Cardinal Mazarin in "The Man in the Iron Mask" (London Adelphi, March - May 1899). A Charles Sugden was living in Bradford in the 1890s. He may be something to Edward Buttenshaw Sugden, 1st Baron St Leonards.

Ceiling detail from Desart Court

On 4th October 1882, Ellen's sister Amelia married another Anglo-Irish noble, Sir Maurice Fitzgerald (1844 - 1916), the 20th Knight of Kerry. His father, Sir Peter Fitzgerald (1808 - 1880), the 19th Knight, had been closely involved with the banking house of La Touche.

It is not clear how much time the 4th Earl and the Countess Ellen spent at Desart. Like his father, the 4th Earl was a man who preferred the country pursuits of shooting and fox-hunting, or indeed, of yachting, to the more mundane business of running an Irish country estate. Indeed Ellen described her husband as "a reckless horseman". At this time, the Desart family estates consisted of approximately 8000 acres in Kilkenny and just under 1000 acres in Tipperary, which yielded £8,932 in 1883. Despite this, the 4th Earl played an active part in introducing the first show of the Royal Agricultural Society to Kilkenny in 1884, and was Master of the Kilkenny Foxhounds from 1882 to 1884. However, shortly after his second marriage the outbreak of the Irish Land Wars once again raised the spectre of politically motivated agrarian violence, and the 4th Earl felt compelled to close up Desart in the winter of 1884 when the family relocated to England for the next 14 years.[33]

On 15th September 1898, less than six months after the death of his mother, the 4th Earl died at the relatively young age of 53-years, after a short illness, on board his yacht off Falmouth.[34] The life of the 4th Earl may have been relatively short but his impact on the family was certainly useful, not least with his acquisition of part of the Bischoffsheim fortunes.

William Ulick O'Connor Cuffe was also a literary man and wrote some fifteen novels during his life. Beginning in 1869 with "Only a Woman's Love", his most successful works were the mystery thrillers *Heme Lodge* (1888) and *The Little Chatelaine* (1889), while his novel *Beyond These Voices* (1870) was a sweeping saga of seduction and revenge set against the background of the Fenian Rising. Other titles included *Children of Nature: A Story of Modern London* (1878), *The Honourable Ella* (1879) and *Lord and Lady Piccadilly* (1887).[35]

His widow, Ellen, Countess of Desart, retired to live with her family at Ascot. Following the death of her brother-in-law, Captain Otway Cuffe, in 1911, she returned to live at Aut Even, near Talbot's Inch, in Kilkenny, where she continued the Captain's good works in the community[36]. She went on to become the first woman Senator in the first Senate of the Irish Free State, and was the first Jewish woman accorded such honours anywhere in the world. She died in 1933 at the age of 75 and was laid to rest by the side of her husband in Falmouth Cemetery.

The life of "Ham" Cuffe, 5th Earl of Desart, is succinctly explained in his autobiographical contribution to his daughter's memoirs, *A Page from the Past*, published by Jonathan Cape in 1940. His granddaughter Iris Origo also provides a charming account of her relationship with him in her own memoirs, *Images and Shadows*, published by John Murray in 1970.

The three sons of the 3rd Earl of Desart were somewhat different in outlook. Where the eldest son, William, enjoyed the leisurely life of a country squire from his youth until his death, Ham Cuffe had a more sober career as

---

[33] Another casualty was the 4th Earl's cousin, the Marquess of Waterford, who awoke at Curraghmore one morning to find his hounds, had been poisoned; the house was closed down and the Marquess moved to England.

[34] GEC, The Complete Peerage Vol. IV (1913) pp. 227 - 231.

[35] John Sutherland, *The Longman Companion to Victoria* Fiction, Longmans (1988).

[36] Ellen and Otway Cuffe, between them had begun a huge number of enterprises namely – they built a theatre, a hospital, a model village with a Woodworkers' factory at Talbot's Inch, a public library, a recreation hall, a woollen mill, a tobacco farm and other co-operative ventures. (*Escape from the Anthill* by Hubert Butler)

one of the leading solicitors in Edwardian England while the youngest brother, Otway Cuffe, was of a decidedly more Celtic temperament and dedicated much of his life to the promotion of the ideals of W. B. Yeats and others, as envisioned by the Gaelic League.

Captain Otway Cuffe (courtesy College Books)

Their early life coincided with a period in which the country houses of the British Isles were in all their glory and, as well-connected young men, they enjoyed every privilege. Shooting weekends with the Duke of Rutland at Belvoir, visits to Paris with Randolph Churchill, dancing to quadrilles and polkas with the Bristols at Ickworth, smoking fat cigars and strolling the sumptuous gardens of Chatsworth with the Devonshires, flirtatious water-parties and archery contests at Longleat were the order of the day.

Ham Cuffe remembered the 1860s as a "very carefree society" in which nobody cared whether one arrived at a garden party "in a donkey-cart or a carriage-and-four". However, following the ill-fated marriage of his brother, the 4th Earl, to Maria Preston in 1871, he does not seem to have visited his childhood home again until he inherited the property in 1898.

He married Lady Margaret Lascelles the second daughter of the Earl of Harewood and they had two daughters but ill-health precluded Margaret Cuffe, Ham's wife from having any further children and so Ham Cuffe would be the 5th and last Earl. His daughters were Joan and Sybil.

The months immediately following the death of the 4th Earl involved a legal dispute with Ellen, the newly widowed Countess of Desart, who initially sought to remain at Desart and run her late husband's estate herself. Ham Cuffe, now 5th Earl of Desart, was equally insistent on returning to his childhood home. In the end Ellen vacated the premises and went to live with her family in Berkshire. Ham Cuffe, his wife and youngest daughter returned to Desart in August 1899. His elder daughter, Joan had married in that year. Her husband was Sir Harry Lloyd –Verney. They had a son who was later to become Major General Gerald Lloyd-Verney and who commanded the 2nd Irish Battalion of the Irish Guards in Italy during the Second World War for which he was awarded the DSO.

The 5th Earl of Desart undertook a major renovation of his family home in County Kilkenny. For the next two decades Ham Cuffe, his wife and their employees were almost perpetually restoring and renovating both house and land, clearing woods and garden borders, fixing new windows, re-hinging gates, attending to dry rot and cracked walls.

Perhaps things became somewhat more manageable when, in accordance with the 1903 Land Act, the 5th Earl sold the bulk of his estate off to his former tenants, retaining just the immediate demesne for himself and his family circle. Nonetheless, his daughter, Lady Sybil, maintained that Ham Cuffe's time at Desart was probably the happiest period of his life and more than compensated for the stresses he had undergone during his time with the Treasury and Department of Public Prosecutions. He adored his new role as country squire, strutting the fields and woods with loyal Spaniel to heel. It was a world Sybil couldn't help comparing to that of The Irish RM - a time of croquet, tennis, picnics and hunting where the Kilkenny people gathered themselves into "a cheerful little company ... farmers on their home-bred hunters, boys on foot or on a donkey's back, a few gentlefolk, a priest or two ... with all that friendly gaiety, could there really be ill-feeling between the races or the classes represented there".[37]

In 1901, Ham's younger daughter, Lady Sybil Cuffe, married a charismatic young American, William Cutting who died young.[38]

---

[37] A Page from the Past, p. 208.

[38] He died on the banks of the Nile in March 1910 with Sybil and 8-year-old Iris in tow.

In 1917 Sybil married secondly Geoffrey Scott (1884-1929), a young architect and writer then working as secretary to Bernard Berenson, the American art historian, at his villa in Settignano. Sybil's marriage to Geoffrey Scott did not last, and the couple divorced.

She remained in Italy, and married thirdly, an old friend Percy Lubbock. Shortly before the outbreak of the Second World War, the couple relocated to a hotel in Vevey, Switzerland and lived amongst the Swiss whom Iris rather bitterly described as "the scavengers of War, more belligerent than any combatant". Sybil was plagued by ill-health, and gradually lost the will to eat. She died on 26th December 1942.

www.ingramcontent.com/pod-product-compliance
Lightning Source LLC
Chambersburg PA
CBHW070023260726
48658CB00003B/1009